A. Alcock

An Account of the deep-sea Madreporaria

Collected by the Royal Indian Marine Survey Ship

A. Alcock

An Account of the deep-sea Madreporaria
Collected by the Royal Indian Marine Survey Ship

ISBN/EAN: 9783337073114

Printed in Europe, USA, Canada, Australia, Japan

Cover: Foto ©ninafisch / pixelio.de

More available books at **www.hansebooks.com**

AN ACCOUNT

OF THE

DEEP-SEA MADREPORARI

COLLECTED BY THE

ROYAL INDIAN MARINE SURVEY SHIP

INVESTIGATOR

BY

A. ALCOCK, M.B., C.M.Z.S., F.G.S.,

INDIAN MEDICAL SERVICE, SUPERINTENDENT OF THE INDIAN MUSEUM AND PROFESSOR OF ZOOLOGY
IN THE MEDICAL COLLEGE CALCUTTA; FORMERLY NATURALIST TO THE MARINE SURVEY.

CALCUTTA:
PRINTED BY ORDER OF THE TRUSTEES OF THE INDIAN MUSEUM.

———

1898.

PREFATORY NOTE.

A good many reports, more or less of a preliminary character, have been published in various Journals since 1885, relative to the zoological work of the Marine Survey of India, under the title of *Natural History Notes from H. M. Indian Marine Surveying Steamer 'Investigator,'* and these unofficial reports have been supplemented since 1892 by the official series—published under the authority of the Director of the Indian Marine—of *Illustrations of the Zoology of the Royal Indian Marine Survey Ship 'Investigator.'*

As the present small volume contains the first independent Report upon a single group of the 'Investigator' collections, it seems advisable to preface it with a short explanation of the way in which the ship became connected with deep-sea exploration and with the Indian Museum.

In the year 1871 the Council of the Asiatic Society of Bengal appointed Dr. T. Oldham, Dr. F. Stoliczka and Mr. J. Wood-Mason to form a sub-committee to report upon the desirability of moving the Government of India to undertake deep-sea dredging in Indian waters.

The sub-committee drew up an elaborate *Memoir* on the subject, in which definite proposals for deep-sea dredging were embodied : this Memoir was submitted to Government, and a copy of it along with a copy of the letter with which it was forwarded, is published in the *Proceedings of the Asiatic Society of Bengal* for 1871.

The Government received the proposals of the Council of the Asiatic Society with cordial approval : it gave a small grant in aid of carrying them into immediate effect, and when, in 1874, the present Marine Survey Department was established, it sanctioned the appointment, upon the staff of the Survey, of a Surgeon-Naturalist—an appointment that had also been strongly advocated by the organizer and first head of the Department, Commander Dundas Taylor, I. N.

But in the early days of the Survey (1874-1881) neither machinery nor vessels capable of deep-sea research were available, so that Surgeon (now Lieutenant-Colonel) J. Armstrong, I.M.S., the first Surgeon-Naturalist of the Department, had to report that it was "quite impossible to carry into "execution the scheme of deep-sea dredging originally proposed by the Council of the Asiatic Society of "Bengal," and had to confine himself to the Zoology of the shallow-water and littoral, although he did manage to dredge in water as deep as 100 fathoms.

However, in 1876, when it had been decided to construct a special vessel for the accommodation of the Marine Survey, the Council of the Asiatic Society again addressed the Government of India, and asked that provision for deep-sea dredging might not be forgotten in the plans for the new vessel. In reply the Government authorized the Council of the Society to confer with the Dockyard authorities on the subject of such equipment.

The Council thereupon appointed a sub-committee, consisting of Dr. John Anderson, then Superintendent of the Indian Museum, and Messrs. J. Wood-Mason (then Deputy Superintendent of the Indian Museum), W. T. Blanford, H. F. Blanford, and H. B. Medlicott, for the purpose of advising the Dockyard authorities in this direction.

The result of this and other measures was that when, in 1881, the new vessel *Investigator* was ready for sea, she was properly provided with the means of undertaking deep-sea research as opportunity should occur.

Before this, however, Dr. Armstrong had left the Survey, and it was not until the end of the year 1884, when Commander A. Carpenter, R. N., was appointed to the command of the ' Investigator,' and Surgeon (now Major) G. M. J. Giles, I.M.S., to the post of Surgeon-Naturalist, that deep-sea dredging became a recognized, if subordinate, branch of the ship's routine.

Since 1885 the Zoological collections made by the ' Investigator' have been steadily accumulating in the Indian Museum, where, in accordance with the recommendations of the Council of the Asiatic Society of Bengal, they have been deposited.

It must not, however, be supposed that deep-sea dredging occupies a very large part of the attention of the officers of the Survey ; since, as a rule, it is only possible when the ship is proceeding to and returning from her systematic surveys of the shores and shallows. It is rarely indeed that as many as twenty deep-sea hauls are made in one year.

From October 1888, when regular records began to be kept, up to the present time, 113 more or less successful hauls have been made in depths of over a hundred fathoms (100-1997 fms.) : of these 71 have been under the superintendence of Captain A. R. S. Anderson, I.M.S., who has been Surgeon-Naturalist since 1893.

As regards the ' Investigator' herself, she is a paddle-steamer of 580 tons, and for a few facts as to her history and equipment I may refer to a paper in the *Scientific Memoirs of the Medical Officers of the Army of India* for 1898.

A. ALCOCK, Major, I.M.S.,
Superintendent of the Indian Museum.

An Account of the Deep-sea Madreporaria collected by the Royal Indian Marine Survey Ship "Investigator."—*By* A. Alcock, M.B., C.M.Z.S., F.G.S., *Superintendent of the Indian Museum and* Professor of Zoology *in the Medical College of Calcutta: formerly Surgeon-Naturalist to the Indian Marine Survey.*

CONTENTS :—

§ I. Introduction.

I include as Deep-Sea Madreporaria only such as have been dredged at a depth greater than 100 fathoms.

Of these we have obtained, during the last ten years, only twenty-five species, of fourteen genera—a small number ; though it must be remembered that the deep-sea dredging operations of the " Investigator " are quite minor incidents of the general practical work of the Survey.

So far as our observations go we find that (speaking, of course, of "deep" forms alone), in the Indian Seas, Madreporaria occur in greatest abundance at a depth of between 400 and 600 fathoms, where the bottom temperature, speaking generally, has been found to range from about 48° Fahr. to about 44° Fahr. Only on one occasion have we dredged corals *in mass* at a greater depth than this, namely at 1,000 fathoms, where the temperature was 38·6° Fahr.

The sea in which corals have been found in the greatest abundance and variety is the narrow basin between the Laccadive and Maldive Islands on the west and the Malabar coast on the east. At one spot in this sea, off the Elicapeni Bank, at 1,000 fms. we dredged over two hundred specimens of a large new species of *Caryophyllia ;* and at another spot, off the Travancore coast, at a depth of about 430 fms., Dr. A. R. Anderson, the present Naturalist on the 'Investigator,' lately dredged "nearly half a ton of living and dead coral......such a haul I have never seen." The corals on this occasion belonged to the genera *Solenosmilia*, *Lophohelia*, *Desmophyllum*, and *Caryophyllia*.

The Andaman Sea ought to be a good place for corals, but it has not yet been sufficiently explored : so far, we have only got six or seven species from it,—and but few specimens of those.

Off the Coromandel coast, in the Bay of Bengal, at a depth of about 600 fathoms, where the bottom-mud begins to harden to a stiffish clay, we have constantly found, in goodly number, *Flabellum japonicum* Moseley, *Flabellum laciniatum* Philippi, and **Bathyactis**; but besides these only two other species, namely a *Caryophyllia* and a **Rhizotrochus**, have been dredged.

§ II. The Geographical Distribution of certain Indian Deep-Sea Corals.

Of the 25 species described in this paper 19 are believed to be peculiar to the depths of the seas of India, although three—or even four—of them have a most suggestive resemblance to certain fossil forms described and figured by Seguenza from the Sicilian Tertiaries.

The remaining six species, which are not peculiar to India, are *Caryophyllia communis*, *Acanthocyathus grayi*, *Flabellum laciniatum*, *Flabellum japonicum*, *Bathyactis symmetrica*, and *Cyathohelia axillaris*.

Of *Acanthocyathus grayi* I can find no other notice than that of its authors, Milne Edwards and Haime, who state that its habitat is unknown.

Of the rest, *Bathyactis symmetrica* is known to have a world-wide distribution, and *Flabellum japonicum* and *Cyathohelia axillaris* are two of the many marine forms that are common to India and Japan.

The remaining two — *Caryophyllia communis* and *Flabellum laciniatum*— may also be taken as furnishing instances of the wide range that a good many deep-sea forms are known to have. But as they are Atlantic species, and are also known as fossils from the Tertiary Deposits of Sicily and Calabria, I think it equally probable that they give confirmatory evidence of the former open sea connexion between the Atlantic and Indian Oceans, by way of the Mediterranean, that geologists believe to have existed in early Tertiary times. As this is a bold theory for such slender *zoological* evidence to support, I must take this opportunity of offering some further corroborative evidence, obtained by summarizing the knowledge acquired by the " Investigator " of the fauna of the Indian Seas at the depths at and near which *Flabellum laciniatum* and *Caryophyllia communis* occur.

Excluding the Foraminifera (of which there are about 280 species) the total number of *named* deep-sea *Metazoa* in the " Investigator " collections is over 600 species, of which about 450 are not known to occur elsewhere, leaving 185 previously-known species.*

Of these 185 species, that also occur in the depths of other seas, (a) thirty-two, or 17 per cent. of them, **belong to the true** abyssal fauna—more than three-fourths of them coming from **depths between 1500 and 1997** fathoms ; (b) **forty,** or nearly 22 per cent. of them, probably belong **to the** nectic fauna ; **and** (c) **a** hundred and thirteen species, or slightly over 61 **per cent.** inhabit the **moderate** depths (between 1000 **and** 100 fathoms—more than **half** of them being found **between 500 and** 100 fathoms) of the slopes.

It is to this last assemblage of species—namely to the fauna of the moderate depths, not far from the coast line, with which *Flabellum laciniatum* and *Caryophyllia communis* are associated, that I wish to invite attention.

[1. Regarding the excluded *true abyssal* fauna (1000–2000 fms.) of these seas, however, I **may** mention that the **32** previously-described abyssal species have the following faunistic relations :—

19 species or 59 per cent. occur in the abysses of the Pacific ;
10 „ „ 31 „ „ „ „ „ Atlantic ;
2 „ „ 6 „ „ „ „ both the Atlantic and the Pacific ;
1 „ „ 3 „ „ „ „ Southern Ocean.

I may further mention that **of the** ten Atlantic species, five are known only from the depths off **the West-Indies and the coasts of** the United States and Brazil. These five **species are** :—

Porcellanaster caeruleus, Wyville-Thomson. ⎫
Pentagonaster intermedius, Perrier.   ⎬ (Asteroidea).
Nymphaster basilicus, Sladen.   ⎭
Pontophilus abyssi, S. I. Smith, (Crangonidæ).
Willemoesia forceps, A. Milne-Edwards. **(Eryontidæ).**

2. **Regarding the** excluded nectic fauna, I may explain that only the following, **among Indian forms, are** counted :—

Gnathophausia, Eucopia, Thysanopoda, Benthenphausia, Petalophthalmus ; Hymenopeneus, Haliporus, Aristeus, Hepomadus, Benthesicymus, Gennadas, Sergestes, Hoplophorus, Acanthephyra, Pasiphæa and *Nematocarcinus*, among Crustacea ; *Onychoteuthis, Callitenthis,* **and** *Cirrhoteuthis*, among the Cephalopod Mollusca ; **and** *Argyropelecus, Sternoptyx, Gonostoma, Chauliodus*, and *Polyipnus*, among Fishes.

* Only the following groups have, up to the present, been named: Hexactinellid Sponges, Madreporaria, Asteroidea, Ophiuroidea, Holothuroidea (partly), Echinoidea (partly), Stalk-eyed Crustacea, Mollusca, Fishes.
Large collections of Octactinaria and Polychæta, as well as small collections of the other marine groups, are still unnamed.

Of the previously-known species of these nectic genera that are found in Indian Seas,

15 species, or 37·5 per cent. of them, are Indo-Pacific;

12 ,, ,, 30 ,, ,, ,, Atlantic;

13 ,, ,, 32·5 ,, ,, ,, both Pacific and Atlantic.]

To come now to the fauna of the slopes, to which *Flabellum laciniatum* and *Caryophyllia communis* belong. This fauna includes 118 (or 61 per cent. of the whole) of the named "Investigator" deep-sea species that are known to occur in the depths of other seas. Of these 113 species 51 per cent. have been dredged by the "Investigator" above the 500 fathom line *only*, and another 13 per cent., though found below 500 fathoms, also range above that limit.

Their affinities with other regions are as follows :—

(*a*) Thirty-three, or slightly over 29 per cent. of them, are found in the West Indies and neighbouring Atlantic coasts from 40° N. to 10° S.;

(*b*) Nineteen, or nearly 17 per cent. of them, occur—including species that are also common to (*a*)—in the Atlantic approaches to the Mediterranean, from Portugal and the Azores to Cape Verde and its islands ;

(*c*) Nine, or nearly 8 per cent. of them, occur—including species that are also common to (*a*) and (*b*)—off the European shores of the North Atlantic ;

(*d*) Twenty-eight, or about 25 per cent. of them, occur—including nine species that are also common to (*a*) or (*b*) or (*c*)—in Japanese Seas ;

(*e*) Thirty-eight, or about 34 per cent. of them, occur—including a considerable number that are also common to (*d*)—in the basins of the East Indian Archipelago ;

(*f*) Fourteen, or slightly over 12 per cent. of them, occur—including forms that are common to some of the other regions—in Australasian Seas (New Zealand, Kermadec Is. and Fiji) ;

(*g*) Six per cent. of them are common to India and the west (Pacific) coast of S. America, especially the neighbourhood of Patagonia ;

(*h*) Two species only (*Cribrella prœstans* Sladen, and *Solariella infundibulum* Watson — the latter also found off the Bermudas) are common to India and the Crozet Islands ;

(*i*) One species (*Metula clathrata* Ad. and Rv.) is known from the Cape of Good Hope ; and

(*k*) One (*Callistephanus koreni* Wright and Studer) from the island of Ascension.

The three following lists illustrate the correspondences, above summarized, between the Indian and Atlantic faunas.

I. *List of Deep-Sea species common to India and the West Indies and neighbouring Atlantic coasts from* 40° *N. to* 10° *S., exclusive of true abyssal and nectic species.* *

Name.	Bathymetric Range in Indian Seas.	Other Localities.
Coelentera		
Farrea occa, **Carter**	220–240 fms.	Philippines, *Japan.*
Aphrocallistes bocagei P. **Wright**	130–265 fms.	N. Atlantic : Spain, Portugal, C. Verde Is. : *Japan.*
Caryophyllia communis, **Seguenza**	210–410 fms.	Atlantic 40° N. to 35° S. : Sicilian Tertiaries.
Cryptohelia pudica, Edw. & **H.**	210 fms.	Atlantic : S. Pacific : *Japan.*
[*Bathyactis symmetrica,* **Pourt.**	600–920 fms.	World-wide range, 32–2900 fms.]
Echinoderma.		
Porcellanaster caeruleus, Wy. **Thoms.**	683–1748 fms.	
Nymphaster basilicus, Sladen	597–1370 fms.	
Ophiomusium validum, Ljungm.	931 fms.	
Ophiernus adspersus, Lyman	490, 683, 719, 1043,1997 fms.	
Ophiocamax fasciculata, Lym.	130–250 fms.	
Astronyx loveni, M. & T.	406 fms.	Northern European Seas : *Japan.*
Crustacea.		
Bathynomus giganteus, A. M. Edw.	696–740 fms.	
Pontophilus gracilis, S. I. Smith	561–683 fms.	
Phoberus caecus, A. M. Edw.	636–931 fms.	(Also Arafura Sea ?)
Uroptychus nitidus, A. M. Edw.	296–636 fms.	
Lithodes agassizii, S. I. Smith	406 fms.	Azores.
Pylocheles agassizii, A. M. Edw.	185 fms.	
Mol. luses.		
Solariella infundibulum, Watson	738 fms.	Crozet Is.
Puncturella asturiana, Fischer	609 fms.	Bay of Biscay.
Octopus januarii, Sstp.	185–271 fms.	Eastern Pacific.
Fishes.		
Chaunax pictus, **Lowe.**	142–400 fms.	Madeira, etc. : *Japan :* Fiji.
Chiasmodus niger, **Johns.**	600–920 fms.	Mid-Atlantic and Madeira.
Bembrops gobioides, (**Goode**)†	128–194 fms.	
Dicrolene introniger, G. & **B.**	406–740 fms.	Atlantic coasts of N. Africa.
Diplacanthopoma brachysoma, Gthr.	400 fms.	
Macrurus cavernosus, (G. & B.)‡	180–405 fms.	
Macrurus laevis, Lowe	188–265 fms.	N. Europe Seas : Madeira : Mediterranean : Hawaii.
Bathygadus longifilis, G. & **B.**	459–740 fms.	Atlantic coasts of N. Africa.
Synaphobranchus pinnatus, **Gray**	459–824 fms.	Azores, Canaries, etc. : Philippines, *Japan.*
Hoplostethus mediterraneus, **C.V.**	145–430 fms.	Atlantic ; Mediterranean : *Japan.*
Polymixia nobilis, **Lowe**	188–405 fms.	Mediterranean approaches of Atlantic : Mauritius : *Japan.*
Antigonia capros, Lowe	296–320 fms.	Madeira : Arafura S. : *Japan.*
Neoscopelus macrolepidotus, **Johns.**	188–405 fms.	Madeira : Australasia.

* To these lists *Ophiomusium planum* Lyman, might almost be added, since although in Indian waters it is an abyssal species, living at 1520–1997 fms., in the West Indies it was dredged at 955 fms. : it has also been dredged off the Azores. I have not included it among the abyssal Atlantic species in a previous paragraph.

† *Hypsicometes parbioides* Goode, belongs to the genus *Bembrops* of Steindachner, and is identical with *Bembrops platyrhynchus* mihi, as I have ascertained by actual comparison with one of the late Mr. Goode's duplicates.

‡ *Bathygadus cavernosus* Goode and **Bean**, is identical with *Macrurus (Hymenocerus) heterolepis* mihi, as I have ascertained by actual comparison of specimens.

II. *List of Deep-Sea species common to India and to the Atlantic approaches to the Mediterranean, exclusive of true abyssal and nectic species.* [*]

Name.	Bathymetric Range in Indian Seas.	Other Localities.
Farrea occa, Carter ...	220–240 fms.	Table I *Japan*, Philippines.
Aphrocallistes bocagei, P. Wright	190–265 fms.	Table I : *Japan.*
Caryophyllia communis, Seg.	210–410 fms.	Table I.
Nymphaster protentus, Sladen	220–250 fms.	
Lithodes agassizii, S. I. Smith	406 fms.	Table I.
Chaunax pictus, Lowe ...	142–490 fms.	Table I : *Fiji : Japan.*
Chlorophthalmus niger, Johns.	690–920 fms.	Table I.
Dicrolene intronigra, G. & B.	406–740 fms.	Table I.
Bathygadus longifilis, G. & B.	459–740 fms.	Table I.
Platytroctes apus, Gthr.	740 fms.	
Leptoderma macrops, Vaillant	753 fms.	
Urocomor cuvieri, Vaillant	430–636 fms.	
Synaphobranchus pinnatus, Gray	459–824 fms.	Table I : Philippines and *Japan.*
Hoplostethus mediterraneus, C. V. ...	145–439 fms.	Table I : Mediterranean : *Japan.*
Polymixia nobilis, Lowe	188–405 fms.	Table I : Mauritius : *Japan.*
Trachichthys darwinii, Johns. ...	206–320 fms.	*Japan.*
Antigonia capros, Lowe	296–320 fms.	Table I : Arafura S. : *Japan.*
Neoscopelus macrolepidotus, Johns. ...	188–405 fms.	Table I : Australasia.
Macrurus laevis, Lowe ...	188–265 fms.	Table I : N. Europe Seas : Mediterranean : *Japan.*

III. *List of Deep-Sea species common to India and the European shores of the North Atlantic, exclusive of abyssal and nectic species.*

Name.	Bathymetric Range in Indian Seas.	Other localities.
Aphrocallistes bocagei, P. Wright ...	190–265 fms.	Tables I and II : *Japan.*
Flabellum laciniatum, Phil. ...	400–600 fms.	Sicilian and Calabrian Tertiaries.
Astronyx loveni, M. & T. ...	406 fms.	Table I : *Japan.*
Enypnyus scaber, Lutk. ...	405–738 fms.	Arctic Seas.
Nephropsis atlantica, Norm. ...	296–740 fms.	
Calocaris macandreae, Bell ...	636–800 fms.	G. of St. Lawrence : New Zealand.
Lucina spinifera, Mont. ...	200–350 fms.	
Puncturella asturiana, Fischer ...	609 fms.	Table I.
Macrurus laevis, Lowe ...	188–265 fms.	Tables I and II : Mediterranean : Hawaii.

We thus see, from the above three lists, that of 113 species inhabiting the moderate depths of the Indian Seas in common with Seas of other parts of the world, no less than 43 are species that also inhabit moderate depths of the

[*] See note * on page 5.

Atlantic north of 10° S., and no less than 38 are identical with species that also belong to the fauna of the West Indies and neighbouring American coasts or of the Atlantic approaches to the Mediterranean.

This, so far as we know, is a larger number of species — speaking only of the fauna of moderate depths below 100 **fathoms** — than the Indian Seas have in common with any one of the Seas that are much nearer and with which they are in much more obvious connexion, namely, the basins of the East Indian Archipelago, the Seas of Japan, and those of Australasia, — as the following three lists will show.

IV. *List of Deep-Sea species, exclusive of true abyssal and nectic species, common to the Seas of India and of the East Indian Archipelago.*

NAME.	Bathymetric Range in Indian Seas.	Other localities.
Aphrocallistes beatrix, Gray	220–240 fms.	
Aphrocallistes ramosus, F. E. Schulze	130–500 fms.	Also Japan.
Cyathelia axillaris, Ed. & H.	88–444 fms.	Also Japan.
Pontaster mimicus, Sladen	1000 fms.	
Ophioglypha æqualis, Lyman	490–1200 fms.	
Ophioglypha undulata, Lyman	675–1132 fms.	
Ophiotrochus punniculus, Lyman	865–1200 fms.	
Pectinura krea, Lyman	865–880 fms.	
Phormosoma bursarium, A. Ag.	636–1070 fms.	Also Japan.
Phormosoma luculentum, A. Ag.	696 fms.	Also Japan.
Arcturus cornutus, Bedd.	490 fms.	
Penæus philippinensis, Sp. Bte.	112 fms.	
Penæus fissurus, Sp. Bte.	133–217 fms.	
Heterocarpus alphonsi, Sp. Bte.	500–740 fms.	Also Japan.
Nephropsis suhmi, Sp. Bte.	890–947 fms.	
Panulirus angulatus, Sp. Bte.	142–400 fms.	
Munidopsis pilosa, Henderson	480 fms.	
Platymaia wyville-thomsoni, Miers	130–340 fms.	
Scyramathia pulchra, Miers	130–561 fms.	
Oxypleurodon stimpsoni, Miers	180–217 fms.	
Amussium caducum, E. A. Smith	410–559 fms.	
Amussium jeffreysi, E. A. Smith	559 fms.	
Modiola teutsoni, E. A. Smith	100 fms.	
Dosinia æstebrosa, Römer	406 fms.	
Cryptodon philippinarum, Hanley	200–350 fms.	
Pleurotoma kieneri, Doumet	180–220 fms.	
Nassa babylonica, Watson	145–250 fms.	
Ranella perca, Perry	100–400 fms.	Also Japan.
Synagrops philippinense, Gthr.	100 fms.	
Sebastes hexanema, Gthr.	188–220 fms.	
Lioscorpius longiceps, Gthr.	185–220 fms.	
Ceratias bispinosus, Gthr.	636 fms.	
Neobythites macrops, Gthr.	188–405 fms.	Also Fiji.
Scopelus engraulis, Gthr.	188–220 fms.	
Malacosteus indicus, Gthr.	650 fms.	
Halosaurus mediorostris, Gthr.	719 fms.	
Symphobranchus pinnatus, Gray	459–824 fms.	Also Tables I and II : and Japan.
Antigonia capros, Lowe	296–320 fms.	Also Tables I and II : and Japan.

Row group labels (left margin): Coelenterata. Echinoderma. Crustacea. Mollusca. Fishes.

V. *List of Deep-Sea species, exclusive of true abyssal and nectic species, common to the Seas of India and Japan.*

	NAME.	Bathymetric Range in Indian Seas.	Other localities.
Coelentera.	Hyalonema apertum, F. E. Schulze	220–240 fms.	
	Farrea occa, Carter ...	220–240 fms.	Tables I & II.
	Aphrocallistes ramosus, F. E. Schulze	130–500 fms.	Also Philippines.
	Aphrocallistes bocagei, P. Wright ..	130–265 fms.	Tables I, II & III.
	Cryptohelia pudica, Edw. & H. ...	210 fms.	Table I : & Atlantic.
	Stephogorgia verrilli, Wright ...	375–409 fms.	
	Flabellum japonicum, Mos. ...	400–700 fms.	
	Cyathohelia axillaris, E. & H. ...	88–444 fms.	
Mol. Crus. Echinoderm.	Pentagonaster arcuatus, Sladen ...	271 fms.	
	Ophioglypha flagellata, Lym. ...	405–675 fms.	
	Ophioglypha imbecillis, Lym. ...	637–800 fms.	
	Astrogyx loveni, M. & T. ...	406 fms.	N. Europe : Japan.
	Phormosoma bursarium, A. Ag. ...	636–1070 fms.	Also East Indian Archipelago.
	Phormosoma luculentum, A. Ag. ...	696 fms.	Also East Indian Archipelago.
	Glyphocrangon hastacauda, Sp. Btc.	669 fms.	
	Heterocarpus alphonsi, Sp. Btc. ...	500–740 fms.	Also Philippines.
	Ranella perca, Perry ...	100–400 fms.	Also Philippines.
	Xenophora pallidula, Rv. ...	100–300 fms.	
Fishes.	Bembrops caudimacula, Stdr. ...	107 fms.	
	Trigla hemisticta, Schleg. ...	98–102 fms.	
	Macrurus parallelus, Gthr. ...	597 fms.	Also New Zealand.
	Halosaurus affinis, Gthr. ...	1600 fms.	
	Chascanor pictus, Lowe ...	142–400 fms.	Tables I & II : & Fiji.
	Synaphobranchus pinnatus, Gray ...	459–824 fms.	Tables I & II : & Philippines.
	Haplostethus mediterraneus, C. V.	145–430 fms.	Tables I & II : & Mediterranean.
	Polymixia nobilis, Lowe	188–405 fms.	Tables I & II : & Mauritius.
	Trachichthys darwinii, Johns.	296–320 fms.	Table II.
	Antigonia cuprea, Lowe	296–320 fms.	Tables I, II & IV.

VI. *List of Deep-Sea species, exclusive of true abyssal and nectic species, common to the Seas of India and Australasia.*

	NAME.	Bathymetric Range in Indian Seas.	Other localities.
Coelentera.	Cinopora tenuis, Mos. [Kermadec Is.]	719 fms.	
	Calypterinus alimani, W. & S. [Fiji.]	703 fms.	
	Ceratoisis grandiflora, W. & S. [Fiji.]	500 fms.	
Echinoderm.	Ophioglypha pallinta, Lym. [S. E. Australia.]	719 fms.	
	Ophiomusium scalare, Lym. [Kermadecs.]	112 fms.	
	Ankyroderma marenzelleri, Thl. [Kermadecs & New Zealand.]	480–500 fms.	
Crustacea.	Penæus rectacutus, Sp. Btc. [Fiji.]	100–250 fms.	
	Iconaxius kermadeci, Sp. Btc. [Kermadecs.]	705 fms.	
	Calocaris macandreæ, Bell [New Zealand.]	636–800 fms.	Table III : & G. of St. Lawrence.

Name.	Bathymetric Range in Indian Seas.	Other localities.
Trachichthys intermedius, Gthr. [New Zealand.]	272 fms.	
Neobythites macrops, Gthr. [Fiji.]	188–405 fms.	Table IV.
Macrurus parallelus, Gthr. [New Zealand.]	597 fms.	Table V.
Bathygadus cottoides, Gthr. (N. Zealand & Kermadees.)	410 fms.	
Neoscopelus macrolepidotus, Johns. [Kermadees.]	188–405 fms.	Tables I & II.

The fact, discovered by the above lists, that so many intimate affinities of the fauna of the moderate depths of the Indian Seas are with the North Atlantic fauna, is so singular as, of itself, to be sufficient to suggest a direct sea connexion, in the past, between the Atlantic and Indian Oceans, and the cases of *Caryophyllia communis* and *Flabellum laciniatum* would indicate that the connexion was by way of the Mediterranean.

Now such a conclusion is in perfect accord with the conclusions of Geology; for there seems to be strong geological evidence (1) that at or about those Tertiary times when *Flabellum laciniatum* and *Caryophyllia communis* lived in the Mediterranean Sea, that sea was in open communication with the West Indian Seas, and also probably extended eastwards as far as Northern Persia and the Red Sea; * and (2) that, at some early part of Tertiary time, seas extended from Europe across the Sahara and Arabia far into India.†

Moreover more than one zoologist has noticed affinities between certain elements of the existing fauna of the Mediterranean and of Oriental Seas and has sought to account for such affinities by a direct open-sea connexion.

For instance, Dr. Günther many years ago discovered the existence of marked affinities between the fish-fauna of the Mediterranean Sea and neighbouring Atlantic waters and that on the one hand of Japan and that on the other hand of the West Indies. References to these interesting affinities are frequent in his writings; and in the *Introduction to the Study of Fishes*, p. 270, he says, in comparing the shore-fishes of Japan with those of the Mediterranean, "we can only account for the singular distribution of these shore-fishes by assuming that the Mediterranean and Japanese Seas were in direct and open communication with each other within the period of the existence of the present Teleosteous Fauna."

---

* Suess, chapter on the Mediterranean, in *Das Antlitz der Erde.* See also J. W. Gregory, *Quarterly Journal of the Geol. Soc.* Vol. II., August, 1895, pp. 255–310.

† Suess, chapter on the Remains of the Indian Continent, in *Das Antlitz der Erde.*

‡ I refer to the French translation of Suess's book, by De Margerie.

In the Journal of the Linnæan Society, Zoology, Vol. xii, (1874–76) the same author gives (p. 108) a list of shore-fishes common to the West Indies, the Mediterranean, and Japan.

Again, Dr. Gwyn Jeffreys in the same Journal of the Linnæan Society, pp. 100–107, gives a list of 1 Brachiopod and 38 Mollusks, both littoral and bathybial, that are common to Japan and the North Atlantic (including the Mediterranean Sea). These are exclusive of several species noted by other authors, and quoted in the said paper, as common to the two regions. Dr. Gwyn Jeffreys, however, seems to think that some of the species may have reached these two remote regions from a common arctic centre of distribution.

In his Report on the "Challenger" Cephalopoda, p. 224, Mr. W. E. Hoyle makes special mention of the occurrence of a Mediterranean species in the Malay Archipelago and Pacific, and briefly refers to the possibility of a former connexion between the Mediterranean Sea and the Indian Ocean.

Finally, the *Geographical Distribution* Chapters and Tables of the "Challenger" Reports are very instructive in this connexion, especially the Table of the Geographical Distribution of the *Echinoidea*, by Professor A. Agassiz.

It appears to me that our facts do necessitate the existence of a direct and open-sea connexion between the West Indian Seas—by way of the islands of the North Atlantic, and the Mediterranean—and the Indian Ocean, since the advent of *Flabellum laciniatum* and *Caryophyllia communis*; and that the analogy of the Alpine floras may fairly be used to explain the occurrence, under similar conditions, of identical species in seas so remote as those of the West Indies and Andamans. In other words, the corresponding species from the East and West Indies may be regarded as the remnant—preserved under corresponding conditions—of the fauna of the single old sea basin, or series of basins of geological speculation.

But, apart from other possible explanations of the occurrence of this large proportion of Atlantic deep species in the Indian Seas, the correctness of our identifications of species may be questioned.

It is therefore necessary to state that the Hexactinellid sponges, including those mentioned in the foregoing lists, were identified by Professor F. E. Schulze, the Ophiuroidea by Professor R. Koehler, the Mollusca (exclusive of *Cephalopoda*) by Mr. Edgar Smith, and the Cephalopoda by Mr. E. S. Goodrich; the Holothuroidea by Dr. J. H. Tull Walsh; the Echinoidea and Crustacea by the late Professor J. Wood-Mason, Dr. A. R. Anderson (the present Naturalist to the Survey) and myself; and the Corals, Asteroidea and Fishes by myself.

As regards my own identifications, five are based on comparisons of specimens from both the regions in question and three more on "Challenger" duplicates from the localities mentioned in Tables IV–VI: the others depend upon figures and descriptions.

III. Descriptions of Species.

The following 25 species are included in this account: the specimens described are in the Indian Museum.

I have here to record my best thanks to Mr. Jeffrey Bell, M.A., for his kindness in comparing duplicate specimens of the *Desmophyllum, Solenosmilia*, and *Lophohelia* here described, with certain types in his charge in the British Museum.

Caryophyllia communis, Seguenza, Moseley.
Caryophyllia ambrosia, n. sp.
Caryophyllia scillaeomorpha, A. A.
Caryophyllia ephyala, A. A.
Caryophyllia paradoxus, n. sp.
Acanthocyathus grayi, Edw. & H.
Trochocyathus retulus, n. sp.
Trochocyathus sp.
Deltocyathus andamanicus, n. sp.
Thecocyathus cincticulatus, n. sp.
Stephanotrochus nitens, A. A.
Stephanotrochus oldhami, A. A.
Desmophyllum vitreum, n. sp.
Flabellum paripavoninum, A. A.
Flabellum laciniatum, Philippi.
Flabellum laciniatum ? var. nov.
Flabellum japonicum, Moseley.
Rhizotrochus crateriformis, A. A.
Lophohelia investigatoris, n. sp.
Amphihelia moresbyi, n. sp.
Cyathohelia axillaris, Ell. & Sol.
Cyathohelia formosa, n. sp.
Solenosmilia jeffreyi, n. sp.
Bathyactis symmetrica, Moseley.
Bathyactis stephana, A. A.

Family TURBINOLIDÆ, Edw. & H., Martin Duncan.

Sub-family *Caryophyllinæ*, Edw. & H.

i. Caryophyllia, Lamk., Stokes, Martin Duncan.

1. *Caryophyllia communis* (Seguenza) Moseley.

Caryophyllia communis, Seguenza, Mem. Accad. Sci. Torino, ser. 2, vol. xxi. 1864, p. 547, pl. v. figs. 7, 7a-c; and pl. xv. figs. 10, 11.
Caryophyllia communis, Moseley, 'Challenger' Deep-Sea Madreporaria, p. 135, pl. i. figs. 4, 5 ; Pourtalès, Bull. Mus. Comp. Zool. vol. vi. p. 100, pl. i. figs. 12, 13 ; A. Agassiz, Three Cruises of the 'Blake' II. p. 148, fig. 462 ; Jourdan, Zoanthaires 'Hirondelle' (Monaco, 1895), p. 12, pl. i. figs. 7, 8.

Four specimens from off the North Maldive Atoll, 210 fms., and a large specimen from off the Travancore coast, 410 fms., are identical with specimens dredged in the Gulf of Gascony by **Dr.** Kochler and his colleagues of the "Caudan" and referred by them to this species. Some young specimens, from the Andamans, 172–303 fms., which I believe to belong to this species, have the base attached to shells, etc. *Distribution :* West Indian Seas, Atlantic between the parallels of 46° N. and 35° S., Arabian Sea. (? Andaman Sea.) *Fossil :* Sicilian (Messina) Tertiaries.

2. *Caryophyllia ambrosia*, n. sp. Pl. i, figs. 1, 1a.

Caryophyllia communis, Alcock, **Ann. Mag. Nat. Hist.** Jan. 1891, p. 6.

This species very closely resembles the preceding, but differs from it constantly (in a series of over two hundred specimens) in the following particulars :—

The calyx is more broadly elliptical in outline and is much more filled up by the septa, pali, etc. : the epitheca is more abundant, and the costæ are much less distinct : the whole texture of the corallum is far more delicate.

The late Professor Martin Duncan, to whom I once sent specimens, wrote that he did "not consider that they belong to Moseley's form *communis* of Seguenza : that has some large costæ—at least, the fossil species which Moseley said his deep-sea forms belonged to has."

Notwithstanding this opinion, I was rashly inclined to believe—especially after seeing the "Blake" figures—that the two forms were identical, until lately when the true *C. communis* was dredged, as above mentioned.

I now think that the present species more closely resembles, and may perhaps prove to be identical with, the *Ceratocyathus suborbicularis* of Seguenza (*tom. cit.* p. 445, pl. v. figs. 6, 6a).

Corallum elegantly horn-shaped, with a thin epitheca which, except in the upper fourth or fifth of the wall, is dull and easily scales off. There are costæ corresponding to all the septa, but they are mere striations, although those of the first two cycles are occasionally a little prominent near the calicular margin —which is broadly elliptical or subcircular.

The septa are all thin and trenchant, with the granular striæ present but inconspicuous. Fourteen to seventeen of them are (equally) large and strongly exsert, and divide the calicle into as many equal chambers; and each chamber is divided into four stalls by three small septa—a median *smaller* and two lateral *larger* and more exsert. Opposite the smaller median septum of each chamber stands a very large thin foliaceous palus, the surfaces of which are strongly denticulate.

There are thus from 14 to 17 large pali, in a crown of remarkable symmetry which largely fills up the calicle.

The columella consists of a large elliptical mass of thin curling ribbon-like processes.

The corallum is pure ivory-white, but often the dull epitheca is discoloured. The soft parts also are quite colourless.

More than 200 specimens, the majority living, were dredged off the Elicapeni Bank (Laccadive Sea) at a depth of 1000 fms., and numerous specimens, further north in the same sea, at 1070 fms.

Unlike so many other deep sea Madreporaria, this species shows a singular constancy of form.

3. *Caryophyllia scillæomorpha*, Alcock. Pl. i. figs. 3, 3a.

Caryophyllia scillæomorpha, Alcock, Journ. As. Soc. Bengal, vol. lxiii. pt. 2, 1894, p. 180.

This species has a striking resemblance to *Caryophyllia scillæ* (Seguenza, Mem. Accad. Sci. Torino, ser. 2, vol. xxi. 1864, p. 442, pl. v. figs. 5, 5a-c.)

Corallum elegantly horn-shaped, with the convexity of the curve somewhat inflated and the apex not corresponding with either principal axis.

Costæ are present—and then are not conspicuous—only near the calicular margin.

The calicle is deep, and its orifice is elliptical—the ratio of the axes as 100: 145. It is divided into fifteen equal chambers by as many large exsert (equal) septa, and each chamber is divided into four stalls by three small septa—a median *larger* with a particularly wavy vertical edge, and two lateral smaller. The surfaces of all the septa have the radiating granular striæ remarkably well developed and regular—like little cockle-shells.

The pali are fifteen in number and are placed opposite the median septum of each of the fifteen principal chambers : like these septa, their free edge is strongly crimped.

The columella is deep-seated and consists of from five to eight elegantly curled ribbons, in a series of remarkable regularity.

The colour of the living corallum is tawny purple outside and white smudged with madder inside.

Off Madras, 107 fms.

4. *Caryophyllia ephyala*, Alcock. Pl. i., figs. 4, 4a.

Caryophyllia ephyala, Alcock, Ann. Mag. Nat. Hist., Jan. 1891, p. 6.

The corallum is goblet-shaped, having a broad encrusting base and a slender cylindrical pedicle which expands rather suddenly into a slightly-curved subcircular or broadly-elliptical cup. It is invested with a very thin vitreous epitheca, and is distinctly costate, to the naked eye, only near the calicular margin.

The septa are in four complete cycles. Those of the first two cycles are large and strongly exsert, and divide the calice into twelve chambers of equal size, those of the third cycle are larger and a little more exsert than those of the fourth and have their very wavy free edge elegantly pleated back, to make room for the large sinuous pali.

The columella is not very deep-seated and consists of several large curled leaf-like processes.

The colour is pure ivory white with a faint brownish-pink tinge near the calicular margin.

Off the west coast of the Andamans, 240–220 fms., and off the Elicapeni Bank (Laccadive Sea) 705 fms.

5. *Caryophyllia paradoxus*, n. sp. Pl. i. figs. 2, 2a-c.

This species is so extremely variable as almost to defy description. Like *Caryophyllia profunda* Moseley, it is found in fused masses encrusting dead coralla; and in one such mass may be found, along with individuals that have the typical Caryophylliaceous corallum, others that have no pali, and hardly more columella than a *Desmophyllum.*

The corallum has an encrusting base and a cylindrical stalk that may be either long slender and twisted or, less commonly, short thick and almost straight. The stalk expands, either gradually or suddenly, into a calyx of which the orifice may be circular, or moderately compressed, or narrowly elliptical with the major axis on a much lower plane than the minor axis; the lip of the calyx may either be everted with the septa exsert, or be not at all everted with the septa not exsert.

The calicle is generally deep, but may be shallow, and the septa pali and columella are not quite alike in any two out of many hundred specimens.

The septa, like the thecal wall, are generally of heavy and coarse make, and have the granules or spicules of the surface so well developed that sometimes they almost meet across the loculi, like synapticula. There are from thirteen to seventeen large, exsert—but never quite equal-sized—septa, which divide the calicle into as many never quite equal-sized chambers, and each chamber is divided into four compartments by three smaller septa—a median, usually large, and two lateral, small.

In the specimens that strictly conform to the *Caryophyllia* type there is a single crown of pali, opposite the middle septum of each of the 13 to 17

chambers. The pali are almost always small and deep-seated, and they are of
every variety of form—thick and spongy, thin and lamelliform, or twisted and
granular. But it is very uncommon to find a crown of pali more often the
pali are mere little ragged lobules of the septa in question, and still more often
they cannot be distinguished at all. Even when there are well formed pali,
they may be absent from some of the chambers.

The columella is generally very deep-seated, and is almost as variable
as the pali : in a few cases a true columella cannot be distinguished ; in many
cases it consists of a single loosely-coiled process, or of two such processes ;
but in most cases it is a good-sized mass, consisting of loosely-connected,
irregularly-twisted, often ragged and granular, processes.

The outer surface of the thecal wall varies greatly in sculpture : sometimes it is only finely striated and granular, but more often fine sharply-salient
but discontinuous costæ, corresponding to the large septa, are present down to
the point where the calyx joins the stalk.

Colours of the "living" corallum : thecal wall, from the point of junction
of the stalk, light brown, gradually darkening to cinnamon near the calicular
margin. The soft parts, in spirit specimens, are dull yellowish.

The zoophytes appear to be extremely prolific, and they thickly encrust
dead corals in colony-like masses connected by copious epitheca. Very often
a young coral is found attached like a bud to the stalk or calyx of a full-grown
one, but, of course, without any internal connexion.

A vast number of specimens were dredged off the Travancore coast, at a
depth of 430 fms., along with almost as much *Desmophyllum* and *Solenosmilia*
and large masses of *Lophohelia*.

ii. ACANTHOCYATHUS, Edw. & H.

6. *Acanthocyathus grayi*, Edw. & H.

Acanthocyathus grayi, Edw. and H., Ann. Sci. Nat., Zool., ser. 3, vol. ix. p. 293, pl. ix. fig. 2, 1848; and Hist. Nat. Corall. II. 22.

A specimen dredged off the Andamans, at 185 fms., seems to me to be
undoubtedly referable to this species, with the description of which it agrees
completely, and from the figure of which it differs only in having longer
spines.

I may mention that in the Indian Museum there are several specimens,
from the Andamans (depth unknown) and from off the Arakan coast (20–70
fms.), which are almost certainly this species, and that in two of them the
spines of the lateral costæ are all flattened and fused together to form a pair of
large wings to the caliele.

iii. TROCHOCYATHUS, Edw. & H., Martin Duncan.

7. *Trochocyathus rotulus*, n. sp. Pl. ii. figs. 1, 1a.

Corallum circular, shallow-saucer-shaped or almost discoidal, with a margin symmetrically scallopped by the exsert septa and costæ.

No epitheca. Thin, sharply granular or spicular costæ radiate from the centre of the disc to the circumference, where they become very prominent.

The septa are very thin and sharp, and have smooth surfaces. Eighteen are pre-eminently large and exsert and divide the calicle into as many equal chambers, each of which is again divided into four compartments by three septa—namely, a median shorter but hardly less exsert than the 18 principal septa, and two lateral which are small and low and soon unite with the median one.

The pali are in two perfectly independent crowns of 18 each: the outer crown are large thin strongly-exsert plates, standing opposite to the median septa of the 18 principal chambers, from which septa they are remarkably well isolated: the inner crown are much smaller and less exsert plates, standing opposite to the 18 principal septa, from which they are separated by deep but very narrow clefts. The surfaces of the large pali (of the outer crown) are denticulate.

The columella is a large irregular spongy mass with a granular and papillary surface.

The corallum is pinkish white, the soft parts are dark purple.

Off North Maldive Atoll, 770-960 fms.

This singularly beautiful species has no close resemblance, except in general shape, to *Deltocyathus*, as I have ascertained by actual comparison.

8. *Trochocyathus* sp.

A second species of *Trochocyathus*, of the same discoid shape but not otherwise similar, was dredged off the Andamans at 185 fms. As there is only one dead and not quite perfect specimen I am unable to determine it.

iv. DELTOCYATHUS, Edw. & H.

9. *Deltocyathus andamanicus*, n. sp. Pl. i. figs. 5, 5a.

Perhaps only a variety of *Deltocyathus italicus* (Michelin).

I have carefully compared the single specimen upon which this species is founded with the descriptions and figures of *D. italicus* of Michelin, Edwards and Haime, Pourtalès, Lindstrom, and Moseley (the figure given by Jourdan in the description of the Prince of Monaco's *Zoantharia* seems to be quite different) and the only differences that I can notice are (1) that, instead of all the costæ being equal, those of the last cycle are much smaller than those of the other cycles (which are all of one size), and (2) that the columella is a little larger, in this species.

Seeing how variable the costæ of *Deltocyathus* may be, and how easily the columella may be affected by more or less fusion with the pali, I doubt whether these differences are specific, and I believe that the form here described may prove to be a variety of *Deltocyathus italicus* (Mich.). If this should be really so, we shall have another connecting link between the West Indian region, the Azores region, the Mediterranean basin and the Seas of India, although, since *Deltocyathus italicus* was dredged by the "Challenger" in the Arafura Sea, this will be no essentially new discovery.

Corallum discoid, free, with a small central scar. Costæ, in their distal half, covered with spiniform granules; those of the first three cycles are indistinct near the scar, but become sharply salient near the circumference; those of the last cycle, which have a ragged appearance owing to the size and abundance of their granules, can be distinguished only near the circumference, and are smaller and less salient than those of the other cycles.

Septa and pali profusely ornamented with spiniform granules. The septa are in six systems and four complete cycles, but in some of the half-systems a fifth cycle is developed.

The septa of the first cycle are large and exsert, and each, with its palus, remains perfectly independent of all the other septa and pali.

The septa of the last cycle are small, independent, and without pali.

The septa of the second and third cycles (and those of the fourth also, in the half-systems in which a fifth cycle occurs) are as large as those of the first, but their pali (which are larger and further from the centre than the pali of the first cycle) soon unite to form "deltas": these "deltas," owing to the size and abundance of their granulation, have a lace-like appearance.

Columella sunken, concave, spongy-papillose.

Colour of the living corallum, madder-tinted.

Diameter of corallum about 18 millim.

A single specimen from the Andaman Sea, 172-303 fms.

v. Thecocyathus, Edw. & H.

10. (?) *Thecocyathus cinticulatus*, n. sp.   Pl. ii. figs. 5, 5a.

This species resembles *Thecocyathus cylindraceus* and *lævigatus* Pourtalès (Ill. Cat. Mus. Comp. Zool. No. IV. 1871, pp. 13, 14) in their somewhat

3

cylindrical shape and in the possession of series of diverticula from the interseptal spaces, which diverticula are not visible externally as rootlets but form
concentric chambers round the inner true limiting wall of the calicular fossa.

The present species also seems to resemble *T. recurvatus* Pourtalès (Bull.
Mus. Comp. Zool. vol. V. 1878-79, p. 202) in its wrinkled epitheca.

It also has a remarkable resemblance to the *Conotrochus typus* of Seguenza
(Mem. Accad. Sci. Torino, (ser. 2) xxi. 1864, p. 477, pl. x. figs. 1, 1*a-d* ; but
there is no doubt about the pali.

The corallum is broadly attached, subcylindrical with a barrel-like bulge,
and somewhat curved, and is smothered in an epitheca so thick and copious
that the edge of the calyx, which just shows clear of it, has a strangled and
swollen look.

The surface of the epitheca is most elegantly ringed or milled, and no
costae show through it, though near the calicular margin shallow grooves
corresponding with all the interseptal spaces do.

The calyx is circular and shallow, being almost filled — somewhat after
the manner of *Heterocyathus* — by the thick close-set and beautifully regular
septa the exsert edges of which are milled.

Nine or ten of the septa are more exsert, but not very much larger, than
the rest, and divide the calicle into as many equal chambers, each of which is
again subdivided into four compartments by three septa of nearly equal size.
The spaces between the septa are mere chinks.

The pali are nine or ten in number and are opposite the median septa of
the principal chambers : they have the form of twisted rods or blunt spires, and
are not very clearly separated from the six or seven similar rods that form the
columella. In addition to the true pali there is an outer crown of almost
paliform thickenings of the edges of the 9 or 10 principal septa.

The colour of the epitheca is french-gray, glistening near the calicular
margin : the septa, etc., are ivory white.

Off the Maldives, 210 fms.

vi. STEPHANOTROCHUS, Moseley.

11. *Stephanotrochus nitens*, Alcock. Pl. ii. figs. 6, 6*a*.

Stephanotrochus nitens, Alcock, Ann. Mag. Nat. Hist., Jan. 1891, p. 7.

Corallum bowl-shaped, heavy dense and stony but not coarse, ivory-white.

The base is gently convex, has a central scar, and is covered with a dull
epitheca: the side-wall, which has a slope of about 85 degrees from the vertical, is free of epitheca. The primary and secondary costae, which radiate from

the central scar, are salient, and are coarse and crenulate on the base, spinate
or denticulate on the side-wall: the costæ of the next two cycles show as striæ
which become indistinct near the middle of the side-wall, though they are
distinct again near the calicular margin.

The calicle is circular and deep. The septa are dense and smooth, and
have trenchant edges: they are in six systems and four cycles, with an incomplete fifth. Those of the first two cycles are pre-eminently large and exsert:
they descend almost to the centre of the calicle, where they end, those of the
first cycle in a single paliform process, and those of the second cycle in two or
three paliform papillæ in linear series, and then they all become loosely fused to
form a small radiculate and papillary columella. The septa of the third cycle are
a good deal larger than those of the fourth: each gives off an uncate paliform
lamella just beyond the middle of its course, but in those half-systems in
which a fifth cycle is developed the tertiary septa are like the secondary septa.
The septa of the fourth cycle are thin crests which do not reach halfway down
the thecal wall, except in the half-systems in which a fifth cycle is developed,
where they resemble the tertiaries.

Of the paliform processes, above described, those of the third cycle are
the largest and form a support for the retracted oral disk.

The soft tissues are very thick and fleshy: the oral disk and tentacles are
very dark purple: the corallum is like the finest unglazed porcelain.

Off the Goa coast, 740 fms.

12. *Stephanotrochus oldhami*, Alcock.

Stephanotrochus oldhami, Alcock, Journ. As. Soc. Bengal, Vol. LXIII. pt. 2, 1894, p. 187.

Corallum bowl-shaped. The gently convex base has a central scar, round
which is a certain amount of dull epitheca: the side-wall rises vertically and
curves outwards again near the calicular margin.

On the base the primary and secondary costæ are very conspicuous and
are coarsely spinate, while those of the other cycles are hardly distinguishable
as granular striæ; but on the side-wall all four cycles of costæ are nearly
equally prominent and are closely granular, those of the first two cycles sometimes having a few teeth.

The calicle is circular and deep, but is a good deal filled up by the septa,
of which there are six systems in four complete cycles with an incomplete
fifth. Those of the first two cycles are pre-eminently large and exsert and
have the surfaces granular: they all end, near the centre of the calicle, in an
upstanding granular paliform process of considerable size, after which they
unite loosely to form a small columella of three or four granular twisted leaflets.

Those of the third cycle unite with those of the second just where the paliform processes of the latter arise. Those of the other cycles are low sharp slightly crenulate ridges, which gradually end low down in the fossa.

The corallum is white with a brownish tinge externally.

Off Pedro Bank (Laccadive Sea), 636 fms.

Subfamily *Turbinolinæ*, Edw. & H.

vii. DESMOPHYLLUM, Ehrenberg, Edw. & H.

13. **Desmophyllum vitreum**, n. sp.   Pl. ii. figs. 2, 2a-b.

Encrusting dead corals in colony-like masses.

The corallum is snow-white with a glistening external surface. From an encrusting base a stout cylindrical slightly-curved stalk of varying length arises and rather suddenly expands into a turbinate calyx, with a spreading lip, the outline of which varies from circular to narrowly-elliptical. Sharpish costæ, corresponding with the first three cycles of septa, are present on the calicular wall only, not on the stalk: the surface between them is generally rippled.

The septa, like the thecal wall, are of a compact porcelain-like texture, and their surfaces are finely and sharply granular. They are in six systems and four complete cycles. Those of the first two cycles are about equal in size, and are large and strongly exsert: they simply meet together and fuse at the bottom of the cup, with hardly any "callus," and sometimes they do not meet at all. Those of the third cycle are a good deal larger and more exsert than those of the fourth: they never fuse with their predecessors, and often descend below the point where the latter fuse. Those of the fourth cycle are small and little exsert, but they descend deep into the cup.

Though the large septa of the first two cycles are described as about equal, no two are of quite the same size, and, in an unbroken specimen, one of them may be found jutting up far above the other eleven.

It is useless to give measurements of such a variable form; an average specimen, picked out at random, is 35 millim. high and has a circular calyx 27 millim. in diameter.

Hundreds of specimens were dredged, along with the *Caryophyllia paradoxus* before described, off the Travancore coast, at 430 fms.

This species appeared to me to be as closely as possible related to *D. eburneum* Moseley, dredged by the "Challenger" off Patagonia at 345 fms.; but Mr. Jeffrey Bell, who has very kindly compared specimens, says "I cannot think that your *Desmophyllum* is the same as *D. eburneum*...... but I am not quite sure that it is not *D. ingens*."

viii. FLABELLUM, Less., Edw. & H., Martin Duncan.

14. *Flabellum paripavoninum*, Alcock. Pl. ii. figs. 3, 3a–b.

Flabellum paripavoninum, Alcock, Journ. As. Soc. Bengal, Vol. LXIII. pt. 2, 1894, p. 187.

Corallum compressed, fan-shaped, with a sessile scar of attachment but no pedicle, and with the two faces somewhat concave.

The lateral costæ are sharp but not salient, they meet the basal scar at an angle of about 45 degrees : the other costæ are merely sinuous striations.

The margin of the calicle is almost entire, and forms a segment of a circle of about 230 degrees ; so that when the corallum is held straight in front of the eyes, with the major axis end on, and without any inclination, the columella—such as it is—is plainly visible above that plane of the calicular margin.

The septa are in six cycles, the last cycle not quite complete ; they are all extremely thin, and have the free edges sharp and straight (not sinuous) and the granular striæ of the surface inconspicuous. Those of the first three cycles are almost equal and meet together at the bottom of the calicle to form a sort of columella by their slightly-thickened ends. Those of the fourth cycle are not so very much smaller than their predecessors, but do not meet them. Those of the last two cycles are small.

Colour of corallum, pale madder, the septa gradually becoming almost white.

Off Pedro Bank (Laccadive Sea) 636 fms.

Height of corallum 39 millim. ; major axis of calicular orifice, 37·5 ; minor axis, owing to the eversion of the rim of the calicle, 30·5 millim.

Judging from Lesson's figure (Illustr. de Zool. pl. xiv.) and Dana's description and figures (U. S. Expl. Exp., Zoophytes, p. 159, pl. vi. figs. 5, 6, 6a) this species is distinct from *Flabellum pavoninum* which has a pedicle, and sinuous septa, the first four cycles of which are equal. At any rate, it is quite as distinct from that species as *Flabellum distinctum* Edw. and H. is.

15. *Flabellum laciniatum* (Phil.) Edw. & H. Pl. ii. figs. 4, 4a.

Phyllodes laciniatum, Philippi Neues Jahrb. f. Mineral. Geol. etc., Stuttgart, IX. 1841, p. 665, pl. xi. fig. B 2
Flabellum laciniatum, Edwards and Haime, Ann. Sci. Nat., Zool., ser. 3, IX. 1848, p. 273 : Hist. Nat. Corall II. 92.
Flabellum laciniatum, Seguenza, Mem. Accad. Sci. Torino, ser. 2, XXI. 1864, p. 485, pl. x. fig. 7.
Flabellum laciniatum, Duncan, Proc. Roy. Soc. XVIII. 1870, p. 293 : Trans. Zool. Soc. VIII. 1874, p. 323, pl. xxxix. figs. 11, 14–18.
Flabellum laciniatum, Lindström, Svensk. Ak. Handl. XIV. pt. ii, 1876, No. 6, p. 12.
Flabellum laciniatum, Wood-Mason and Alcock, Ann. Mag. Nat. Hist., Dec. 1891, p. 450, fig. 15.

Corallum extremely thin and fragile, elegantly fan-shaped with a well-defined but short scar-like pedicle, the calicular margin deeply cut into twelve deeply-laciniate leaves, two of which—namely those at either end of the major axis—are thin almost horizontal wing-like expansions formed of a principal septum and its corresponding thin foliaceous costa (the " lateral " costæ).

The two faces of the corallum are quite flat (that is, not in any way curved) and each is traversed by five broad low costæ, corresponding with the septa of the first two cycles, between which are the less distinct costæ of the third and, sometimes, of the fourth cycles. The costæ and the spaces between them are regularly marked with ripple-like growth-lines.

The septa are in six systems and four complete cycles, with an incomplete and inconspicuous fifth. Those of the first two cycles are pre-eminently large and, with those of the fourth cycle, form the jagged middle lobes of the twelve leaves above-mentioned. Those of the third cycle are much larger than those of the fourth but are not nearly so far exsert. The surfaces of the septa are much wrinkled or cockled, the convexities of the wrinkles being finely spicular.

The columella, such as it is, is formed by the fusion, in the very bottom of the calicle, of the first three systems of septa.

The fresh corallum, like the living polyp, is of a dark madder colour, but the dry corallum fades.

This species is one of the common inhabitants of the Indian Seas at depths of 400 to 600 fms. We have dredged it in the Andaman Sea, at several places in the Bay of Bengal, and at several places in the Laccadive Sea. It appears to prefer soft muddy bottoms.

As the late Professor Martin Duncan remarked, the corallum is so fragile that it is sometimes broken by the postmortem contraction of the soft parts. Dr. A. R. Anderson, the present Surgeon-Naturalist with the " Investigator," has, however, had the good fortune to dredge some perfect specimens, one of which is now figured.

I have carefully compared our specimens with the original figures and description of Philippi and with Seguenza's figures, and I feel no doubt about the identity of our species with theirs. But I do not feel the same certainty with regard to Martin Duncan's figures.

In the synonomy of this species *Ulocyathus arcticus* Sars (" Reise i Lofodden, p. 21; and Faun. Lit. Norv. 2 heft 1856, p. 73, pl. x. figs. 8-27 ") is included by Martin Duncan and Lindström : I have not seen the papers referred to. Lindström also includes (1) *Flabellum MacAndrewi* Gray (P. Z. S. 1849, p. 75, Radiata, pl. ii. fig. 11) which is founded on fragments the figures of which are insufficient for comparison, and (2) *Flabellum alabastrum*, Moseley (" Challenger " Deep Sea Madreporaria, p. 169, pl. vii. figs. 1, 1*a-b*, 2, 2*a-b*, and pl. xvi. fig. 11). I can only say that I have examined a large number of specimens of *Flabellum laciniatum*—including a series of over twenty almost perfect specimens varying from 15 millim. to 51 millim. in major diameter—and that they show practically no variation; so that I think Moseley's species is distinct.

Distribution : Norwegian and North Atlantic Seas ("a common form"—Duncan), Indian Seas at 400–600 fms. (a common inhabitant). *Fossil :* Calabrian and Sicilian Tertiaries.

16. ? *Flabellum laciniatum*, var.

In the Andaman Sea, 172–303 fms., there was dredged a single small living specimen that resembles *Flabellum laciniatum* in everything, except that the ten large septa of the first two cycles that spring from the faces of the thecal wall are not sufficiently exsert to cut the calicular margin into the petaloid lobes that are so characteristic of *F. laciniatum.* The corallum thus looks like that of a *F. laciniatum* which has had all these lobes broken off, leaving only the wing-like lateral costæ and their corresponding septa intact.

In colour, texture and all other respects it corresponds with *F. laciniatum*, and except that its pedicle is attached to a small shell, it might, at first sight, be taken for a damaged specimen of that species.

Major diameter of calicle 26 millim.

17. *Flabellum japonicum*, Moseley.

Flabellum japonicum, Moseley, 'Challenger' Deep Sea Madreporaria, p. 169, pl. vii. figs. 3, 3a, pl. xvi. fig. 12.
Flabellum japonicum, Wood-Mason and Alcock, Ann. Mag. Nat. Hist., Dec. 1891, p. 449.

This also is one of the common inhabitants of the Indian Seas at depths between 400 and 700 fms. It also seems to prefer a muddy bottom. It reaches a large size: in the Indian Museum we have one specimen which measures 3 inches by 2¼ inches in the diameters of the calicular orifice, and several that approach this size.

It varies a good deal in shape, in costal sculpture, and in the development of the columella. In young specimens the corallum is wide and shallow, with a distinct pedicle, with the costæ of the first two cycles sharply prominent, and the columella loose and comparatively large.

In old specimens the corallum is somewhat compressed, the calicle is deep, the pedicle is a mere blunt point, the columella is a small plug of dense tissue, and the costæ of the first two cycles are either sharply prominent or inconspicuous.

Distribution : Japanese and Indian Seas at about 400 fms.

ix. Rhizotrochus, Edw. & H., Martin Duncan.

18. *Rhizotrochus crateriformis*, Alcock.

Rhizotrochus crateriformis, Alcock, Journ. As. Soc. Bengal, Vol. LXII. pt. 2, 1893, p. 170, pl. viii. figs. 1, 2; and Vol. LXIII. pt. 2, 1894, p. 187.

Only four specimens have been dredged, and three of them are impacted in dead coralla of their own species, which has caused great irregularity of growth. The description applies to a clean free specimen dredged off the Coromandel coast at a depth of 573 fms.

The corallum is low, bowl-shaped, having a small central mamillary scar, a very thin fragile thinly-epithecate wall, and a circular orifice with the lip gently everted. (In the impacted specimens the calicular orifice is, in a general way, broadly-elliptical, but is about as irregular as it can be).

From the thecal wall, which is marked with close faint longitudinal and transverse striæ, a few large cylindrical rootlets stand out at a wide angle.

The septa are in four complete cycles and an incomplete and inconspicuous fifth: at, and for some considerable distance below, the calicular margin they are mere ridges, but comparatively low down in the calicle they jut out strongly, so much so that in the case of the first three cycles they look almost like large pali: they are thin and have sharp edges, and their surfaces are marked with concentric lines of granules or spicules. The septa of the first two cycles are about equal—though there is no complete uniformity among them—and are not very greatly larger than those of the third cycle—though there is considerable irregularity of size in this cycle also. All three cycles meet at the bottom of the calicle to form a sort of trabecular columella : above this they leave a wide clear space. The septa of the fourth cycle are very much narrower than most of those of the third.

Colour in spirit—both of corallum and of soft parts—white.

The type was dredged on a muddy bottom off the Coromandel coast at a depth of 573 fms. Subsequently 3 large specimens were dredged off Madras at the very different depth of 33 fms.

The principal septa sunken below the calicular margin gives this species a remarkable appearance.

Family OCULINIDÆ, Edw. & H., Martin Duncan.

x. Lophohelia, Edw. & H.

19. *Lophohelia investigatoris*, n. sp. Pl. iii. figs. 1, 1a–b.

Corallum in irregularly ramifying colonies, but proceeding by regular alternate distichous subterminal gemmation, occasionally dichotomous.

The surface of the branches is quite smooth to the naked eye, but round that part of the margin of the cups that is not immersed in the base of their successor faint traces of costæ may sometimes be seen with a lens.

The cups are circular, deepish in the living state, and empty-looking— owing to the scarcity and tenuity of the septa.

The septa, which are not at all exsert, are in six systems and three cycles, but those of the third cycle need careful looking for with a lens. Even those of the second cycle are often small and inconspicuous. Those of the first cycle are always plainly visible to the naked eye: even they are often inconspicuous near the mouth of the cup, but deeper down, where they meet, they are pro- minent.

There is no columella: the septa often barely meet.

As growth proceeds, several more or less parallel branches may fuse to- gether, not in a solid mass but by a superficial crust, and in this way hollow branching trunks result, which give a lodging to a large species of polychæte. Furthermore, as these trunks age, the calices on their surface fill up, and at last show as mere smooth round depressions.

The colour of the fresh corallum varies from light pinkish brown to cinnamon. Diameter of calices 3 to 4 millim.

A large number of branches was dredged off the Travancore coast at 430 fms.

This species seems to be nearest to *Lophohelia candida* Moseley, which was dredged by the "Challenger" in the West Indian Seas at 450 fms.

xi. AMPHIHELIA, Edw. & Haime, Martin Duncan.

20. *Amphihelia (Diplohelia) moresbyi*, n. sp.   Pl. iii. figs. 4, 4*a*.

Corallum proceeding by regular alternate-distichous, sometimes dichotom- ous, subterminal gemmation.

Surface of branches quite smooth to the naked eye, extremely faintly granular and striated under the lens: at the very margin of the calicles are short costal ridges corresponding with the septa.

The calices are sub-circular and deep, and their cavities are very little encroached upon by the narrow septa: these are in six systems of three com- plete cycles, are *almost all of one size*, and are slightly exsert; their surfaces are roughened by small spicules.

There is a deep-seated spongy-trabecular columella of some size, but there are no pali.

Colour white. Diameter of calices 4 millim., or a little less.

4

Unfortunately the label of these specimens has been lost, but I know that they came either from off the Konkan coast or from off the Laccadives, and from a depth not less than 444 fms.

This species is characterized by the remarkably uniform size of the septa.

Named in memory of Captain Moresby of the Indian Navy, a marine surveyor whose work in these seas is well known through Darwin's "Coral Reefs."

xii. CYATHOHELIA, Edw. & H., Martin Duncan.

21. *Cyathohelia axillaris*, (Ell. & Sol.).

Madrepora axillaris, Ellis and Solander, Nat. Hist. of Zoophytes, p. 163, pl. xiii. fig. 5.

Cyathohelia axillaris, Edwardes and Haime, Hist. Nat. Coralliaires, II. 110: Duncan, P. Z. S. 1876, p. 438; Moseley, Challenger Deep Sea Madreporaria, p. 175.

A small, undoubtedly "living," branch, together with a dead one, was dredged with numerous living branches of the last-mentioned species, off the Malabar coast, probably at 444 fathoms, or at a still greater depth.

This coral had also been dredged off Madras, at 88 fms.

Our specimens are identical with some in the Indian Museum from Japan.

Distribution: Japan and Moluccas, Bay of Bengal, Malabar Sea.

22. ? *Cyathohelia formosa*, n. sp.   Pl. iii. figs. 2, 2a.

This species appears to be a *Cyathohelia* although some of its branches do not exhibit the characteristic gemmation of that genus, and although the *two* crowns of pali are not distinctly recognizable and the septa are fewer.

In typical branches the gemmation is regularly dichotomous, and leaves the parent calice immersed between, but not very much compressed by, the bases of its pair of successors.

The surface of the branches is snow-white and perfectly smooth to the naked eye, though under a lens it is finely frosted and sometimes, but not always, finely striated.

The free cups are circular and moderately deep and have an edge slightly scalloped by the moderately exsert septa, which do not much fill up the fossa.

The septa are in six systems and three cycles. Those of the first two cycles are equal in size, and opposite to each one of them is, generally, a large twisted foliaceous palus. But the pali are very irregular in size, and one or two are occasionally absent. The septa of the third cycle are small and independent throughout their visible course: it occasionally happens that a little palus may stand opposite to a single *one* of them.

The columella is variable: sometimes it consists of a few thin twisted ribbons which in places are confluent with two or three of the pali, sometimes it consists of a few papilliform lamellæ; it is always small.

The colour both of soft parts and of corallum is white.

The diameter of an average (parent) calicle is about 3 millim.

Dredged along with a beautiful little species of *Cryptohelia*, off the Maldives at 210 fms.

Though not a typical *Cyathohelia*, this species seems to me to be nearer to this genus than to either *Bathelia* or *Sclerohelia*.

xiii.   SOLENOSMILIA, Martin Duncan.

23.   *Solenosmilia Jeffreyi*, n. sp.   Pl. iii. figs. 3, 3a–b.

Corallum dendroid, the terminal calyces of the branches having the typical form—*i.e.*, two calyces imperfectly separated by fission, with a common fossa and columella; though it may happen that four or even eight calyces may communicate, in which case there is no columella.

In the distal halves, more or less, of the branches, large rugiform costæ— which are few in number and are somewhat twisted—are present; but the older parts of the branches have a smooth frosted appearance.

The *primary calyces* are usually subcircular, with a deep fossa, and with three complete cycles—and an incomplete fourth cycle—in six systems, of thin septa. The septa are of no great breadth and do not much encroach on the fossa: though there is often a want of uniformity among them, no one system is of markedly predominant size: they are sometimes straight, sometimes twisted, and their surface is variably spicular. The columella is usually deep-seated, and usually consists of a light-looking mass of thin loosely-twisted processes.

The *calyces in and after recent fission* are of every shape, from elliptical to polygonal: large wrinkle-like costæ are present, the septa are rather capricious in size and form, and the columella is often so deep as to be invisible. In some cases no columella is present, and then the end of the branch for some distance is quite hollow, so that the fossæ of several corallites or pairs of corallites are in widely open communication.

The colour of the "living" corallum varies, from cinnamon in the older parts, to yellowish brown in the parts newest formed.

An immense mass, living and dead, was dredged off the Travancore coast at 430 fms.

I took this to be *Solenosmilia variabilis* Duncan, but Mr. Jeffrey Bell, who has kindly compared the two, says "they may be the same, but the calicles of your species are larger, and there is more anastomosis of the several tunnels. I think they should be kept apart."

Family FUNGIDÆ, Dana.

Subfamily *Lophoserinæ*, Edw. & H.

xiv. Bathyactis, Moseley.

24. *Bathyactis symmetrica*, (Pourtalès) Moseley.

Fungia symmetrica, Pourtalès, Ill. Cat. Mus. Comp. Zool. No. IV. 1871, p. 46, pl. vii. figs. 5, 6: Martin Duncan, Trans. Zool. Soc. VIII. 1874, p. 334, pl. xlix. figs. 16–19.

Bathyactis symmetrica, Moseley, Challenger, Deep Sea Madreporaria, p. 186, pl. xi. figs. 1–13: Wood-Mason and Alcock, Ann. Mag. Nat. Hist. Jan. 1891, p. 8: Jourdan, Zoanth. "Hirondelle" (Monaco, 1895), p. 28.

This species has been dredged by the 'Investigator' in the Bay of Bengal, off the Coromandel Coast, at 920–690 fms., and in the Arabian Sea, off the Maldive Is., at 719 fms.

I identify it with the beautiful figures of Moseley's Report. It was discovered by the U. S. Survey in the West Indian Seas at depths of 450 and 350 fms., and seems to have been constantly found afterwards in those seas at depths of 100 to 805 fms. By the "Challenger" it was met with in many places in the North and South Atlantic, the South Indian Ocean, and the East and West Pacific, and was found to have a bathymetrical range of 32 fms. to 2900 fms.—"a wider range in depth than any other animal" (Moseley), and "a world-wide distribution" (Wyville Thomson).

25. *Bathyactis stephana*, Alcock. Pl. iii. figs. 5, 5*a*.

Bathyactis stephanus, Alcock, Journal Asiatic Soc. Bengal, Vol. LXII. pt. 2, 1893, p. 149, pl. v. figs. 12, 12*a*.

The chief differences between this species and the preceding are that the base of the corallum is strongly concave, making the upper surface of the corallum strongly convex, and that the septa of the first three cycles are foliaceously expanded to a remarkable height and have their edges, when unbroken, entire (very finely denticulate when magnified).

The corallum is very thin and fragile, circular, strongly convex, the base forming an inverted bowl. The costæ radiate from the centre like the spokes of a wheel, and become sharply cristiform as they approach the circumference.

Septa in six systems and five complete cycles, arranged exactly as in *B. symmetrica*, that is to say, the primary septa are independent, while those of

29

the other cycles unite, with beautiful regularity, in such a way as to form series of deltas in each of the six principal chambers. Those of the first three cycles are in the form of large upstanding leaves, and though their surfaces are regularly wrinkled like cockle-shells, their free edges are entire.

Synapticula in ten to twelve zones, which though forming fairly regularly concentric series, do not at once arrest the eye by this character.

Columella distinct. Corallum brilliant white: soft parts mauve.

Bay of Bengal, off the Kistna Delta, 678 fathoms, and off Trincomalee, 800–636 fms.

The form and structure of the septa in this species is much like that of the *Stephanophyllia imperialis* figured by Michelin (Icon. Zoophytol. pl. viii. fig. 1*a*).

EXPLANATION OF PLATE I.

Figs. 1, 1a. *Caryophyllia ambrosia*, × 2.

Figs. 2, 2b. *Caryophyllia paradoxus*, natural size.

Figs. 2a, 2c. *Caryophyllia paradoxus*, × 2.

Figs. 3, 3a. *Caryophyllia scillæomorpha*, × 3.

Figs. 4, 4a. *Caryophyllia ephyala*, × 4.

Figs. 5, 5a. *Deltocyathus andamanicus*, × 2.

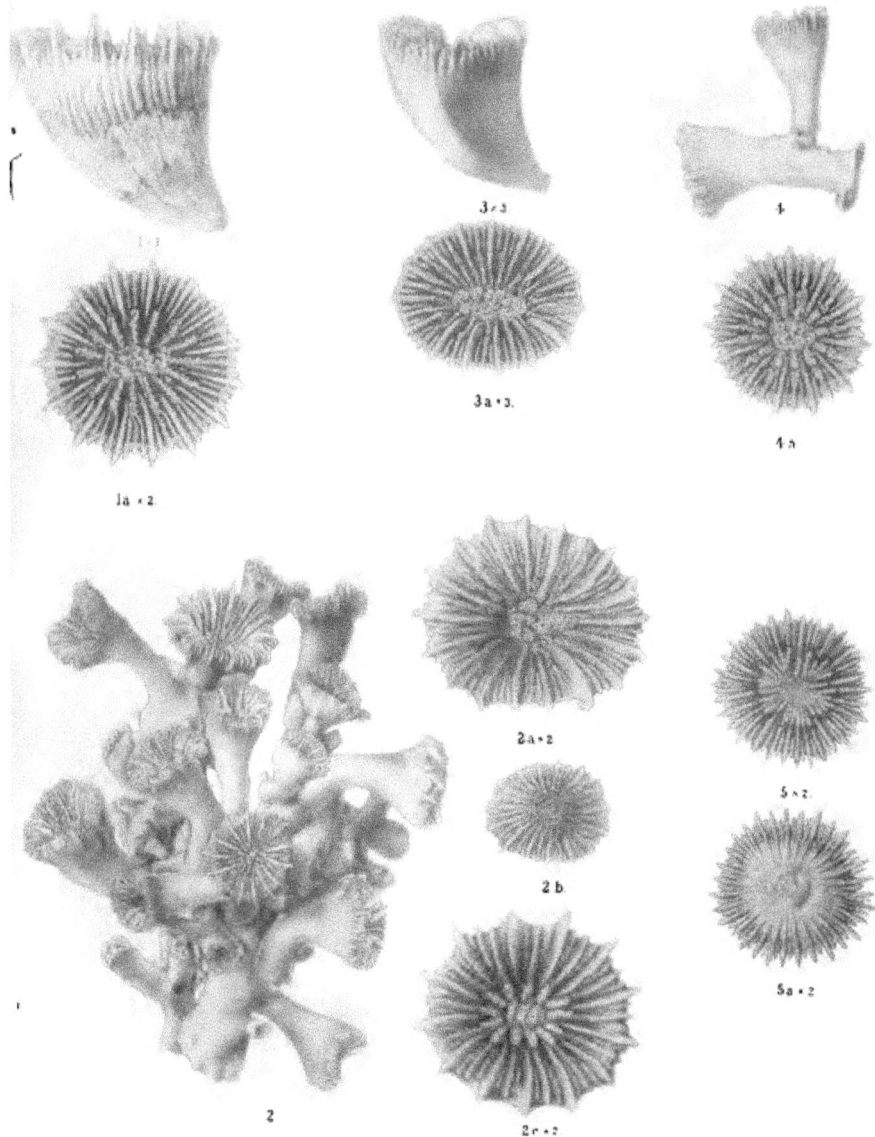

1. Caryophyllia ambrosia   2 Caryophyllia paradoxus   3 Caryophyllia scillaeomorpha
4 Caryophyllia ephyala   5 Deltocyathus andamanicus

EXPLANATION OF PLATE II.

Figs. 1, 1a.   *Trochocyathus rotulus* × 2.

Fig. 2.   *Desmophyllum vitreum*, natural size.

Figs. 2a, 2b.   *Desmophyllum vitreum*, × 2.

Figs. 3, 3a, 3b.   *Flabellum paripavoninum*, natural size.

Figs. 4, 4a.   *Flabellum laciniatum*, Phil., natural size.

Figs. 5, 5a.   *Thecocyathus cincticulatus*, × 3.

Figs. 6, 6a.   *Stephanotrochus nitens*, natural size.

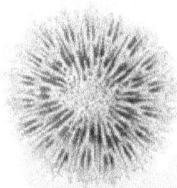

5a × 3.

6

5 × 3.

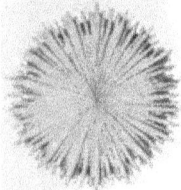

1a × 2.

6a.

2a × 2.

2b × 2

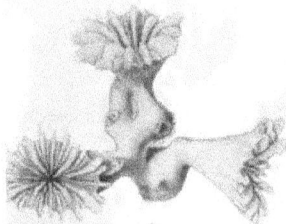

2.

3a.

3b

3

4.

EXPLANATION OF PLATE III.

Fig. 1.   *Lophohelia investigatoris*, natural size.

Figs. 1a, 1b. *Lophohelia investigatoris*, × 9.

Fig. 2.   *Cyathohelia formosa*, × 2.

Fig. 2a.   *Cyathohelia formosa*, × 8.

Fig. 3.   *Solenosmilia jeffregi*, natural size.

Figs. 3a, 3b. *Solenosmilia jeffreyi*, × 4.

Fig. 4.   *Amphihelia moresbyi*, × 2.

Fig. 4a.   *Amphihelia moresbyi*, × 8.

Figs. 5, 5a. *Bathyactis stephana*, × 1½.

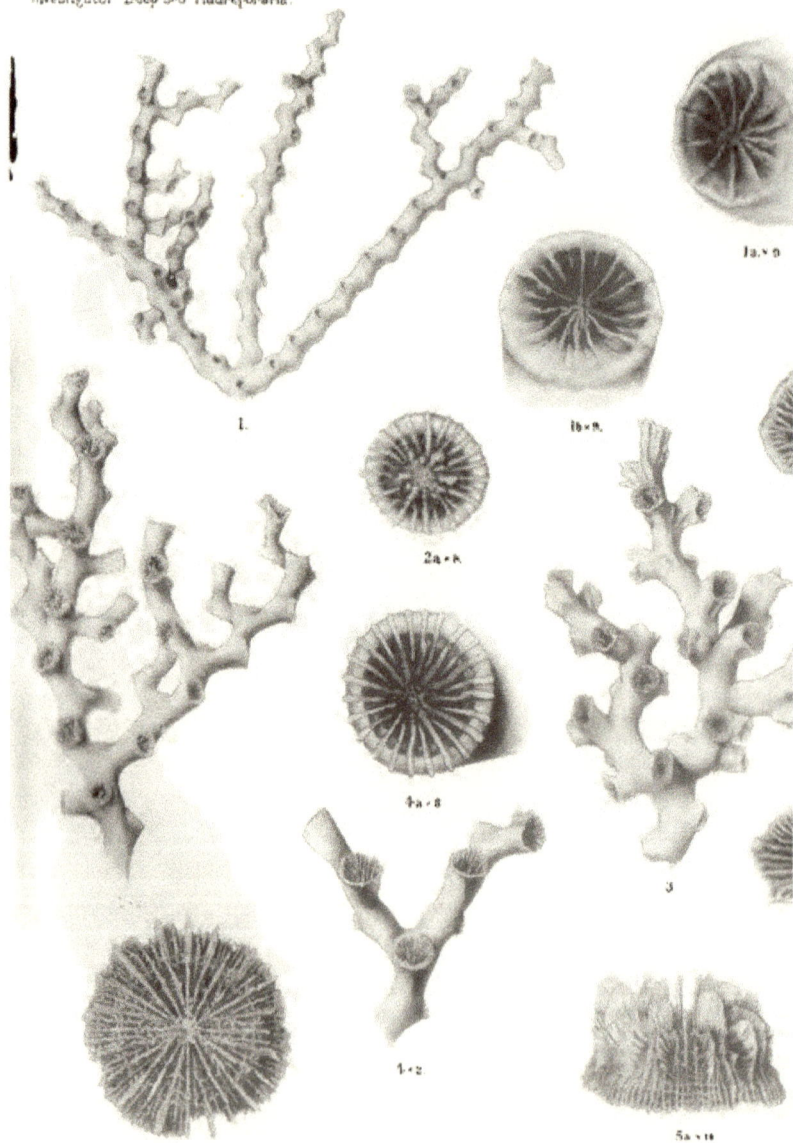

1.

1a × 9

1b × 9.

2a × 8

4a × 8

3

1 × 2

5a × 10

www.ingramcontent.com/pod-product-compliance
Lightning Source LLC
Chambersburg PA
CBHW021441090426
42739CB00009B/1586